Body Facts

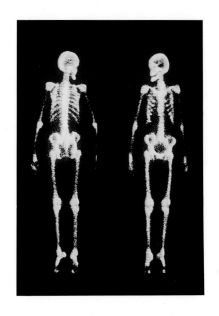

David Drew

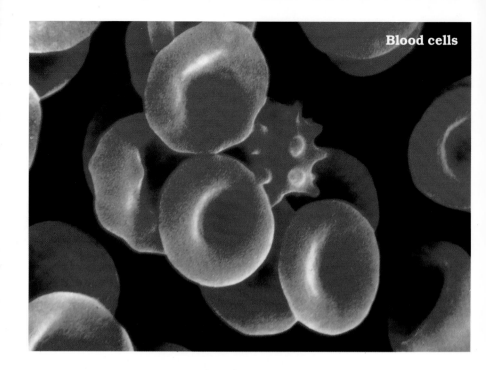

Blood cells

Contents

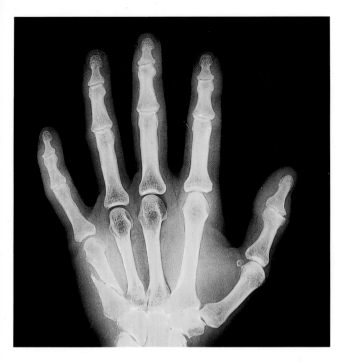

Inside your hand are 27 bones. Each finger has three bones, but your thumb has only two. The other thirteen bones are in your palm.

What's inside me?

Inside your body are
- 206 bones,
- more than 600 muscles,
- 60,000 miles of blood vessels, and
- 50,000 million cells.

☞ You have more cells in your body than there are people on the Earth.
☞ Your blood vessels are long enough to circle the Earth twice.

Baby bones
When you were born, you had 100 more bones than you have today.
Many of these bones join up as you grow bigger.

Inside one of your blood vessels can be seen red cells, white cells and platelets. A single drop of blood the size of a pin head contains 5 million red cells, 10,000 white cells and 200,000 platelets.

Why do I bleed?

Your blood is half liquid (called plasma) and half blood cells, which carry oxygen to all parts of your body. When you cut yourself the plasma flows out, along with the blood cells. The blood is pushed out by the pumping of your heart.

The heart pump

Your blood is moved around your body by the pumping action of your heart. You can feel this pumping as your heart beating. In one day your heart beats 100,000 times.

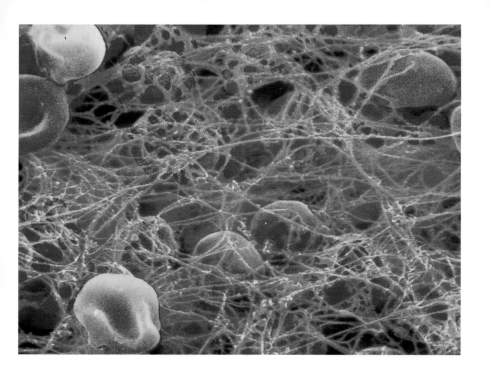

How does the bleeding stop?

Soon after you start bleeding, some of the platelets in your blood join together. They produce tiny threads at the opening of the cut. These sticky threads form a net that traps the cells so they can't escape.

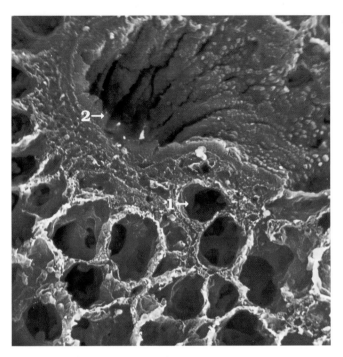

Your lungs have millions of air pockets called alveoli (1). Tiny blood vessels called capillaries form a net around each air pocket. Fresh air is carried to them by small tubes called bronchioles (2).

Why must I breathe?

Every time you breathe in, your lungs fill with air. One-fifth of the air is oxygen. Millions of air pockets in your lungs pass the oxygen into your blood ...

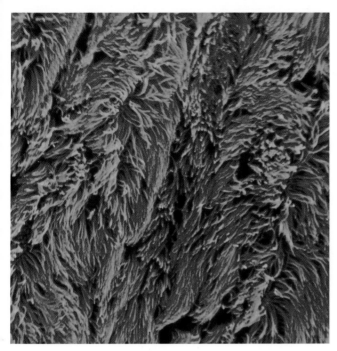

Inside your throat is your windpipe. Inside your windpipe, the walls are covered with fine hairs like a carpet.

The blood then carries the oxygen to your muscles, which use up the oxygen when they work for you. Without oxygen your body would stop working.

How often do I breathe? Count the number of normal breaths you take in one minute. Most people take about 12 breaths in that time. This means you breathe in 17,000 times a day, or more than 6 million times a year.

The tiny hairs that line your throat are called cilia. The cilia help clean the air you breathe. They beat back and forth like the oars of a boat, sending the dust up your throat so it can be breathed out again or swallowed.
You have these hairs inside your nose as well.

What makes me cough?

Every time you breathe in, thousands of tiny specks of dust and pollen are sucked into your throat. Many of them are caught among the hairs that line your windpipe ...

Why do I breathe faster when I'm running?
The more energy you use, the more your muscles need oxygen. After a race, you need more than 100 breaths a minute, which amounts to 800 pints of air.

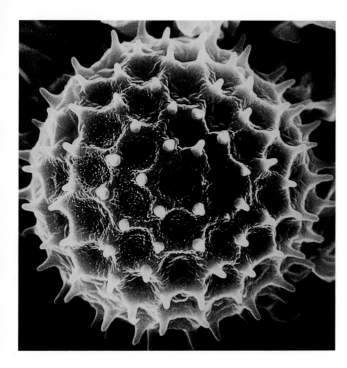

Pollen grains are made inside flowers. They are the specks of yellow dust you get on your fingers when you rub the center of a flower.
This pollen grain is from a Blue Dawn flower.

Sometimes a grain of pollen gets stuck in this carpet of hairs. The sharp points of the pollen touch nerves that tell your brain to organize a cough.

The brain tells the throat to close off while pressure builds up in your lungs. This pressure forces air up your throat, taking the pollen with it and making a loud noise — your cough.

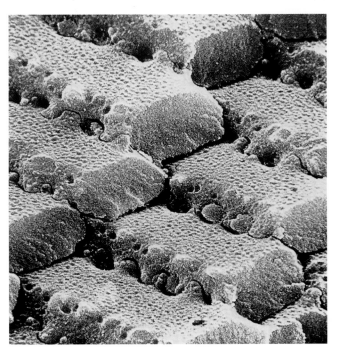

The lens of your eye is made of millions of flat cells arranged neatly in rows. The ten cells in the picture have been magnified 5,000 times.

Why do I blink?

The surface of your eye has a thin layer of skin cells that are very sensitive to dust falling on them. When you blink, your eyelids wash over the surface of the eye with a fluid that clears the dust away.

How much time do I spend blinking?
A blink lasts less than half a second. But if you add up all the blinking you do in a day, it would equal 30 minutes. So that makes half an hour a day when you can't see anything.

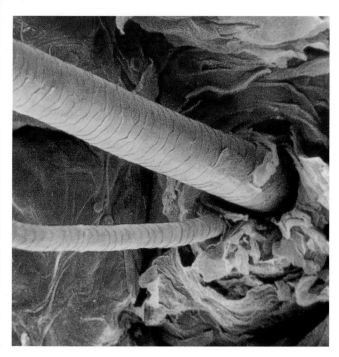

Two hairs emerging from your skin. Your body has about two million of these hairs.

When I cut my hair, why doesn't it hurt?

There are two parts of your body that feel no pain: your hair and your nails. They are mostly made of dead cells. So if you cut a hair it cannot send any pain messages to your brain.

But if I pull a hair it hurts. Why?
The only living part of a hair is the hair's root under the skin. When you pull a hair, it is the hair's root that feels the pain. The root sends its cry for help along a nerve to your brain.

11

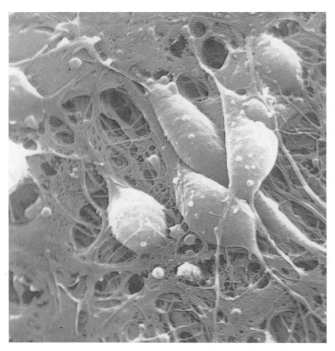

These are just a few of the nerve cells that make up the "gray matter" in your brain. These cells receive messages from other parts of your body. They also send out instructions. Your brain exchanges millions of pieces of information every minute.

What's inside my brain?

Your brain is packed with 10 million nerve cells. Each cell has fibers that link it with other nerve cells all over your body. Your brain can think in more ways than the world's largest computer, yet it is 80% water.

Two brains in one?
Your brain is divided into two halves. You use the left side of your brain when you speak or solve problems in mathematics. You use the right side when you play music, draw a picture, or invent things.

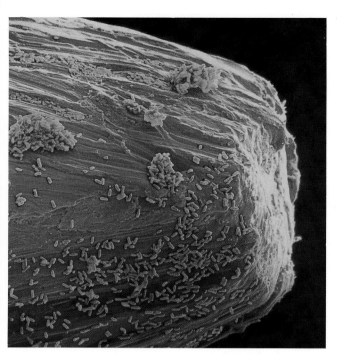

How many bacteria are at the sharp end of this pin?

How big is a cell?

Your whole body is made of cells. It also contains visiting cells that enter through your nose and mouth. Some of these cells are bacteria — the "germs" that sometimes make you sick. The bacteria cells in the picture are clinging to the sharp end of a pin. A row of at least 50 bacteria cells would be only one sixteenth of an inch long.

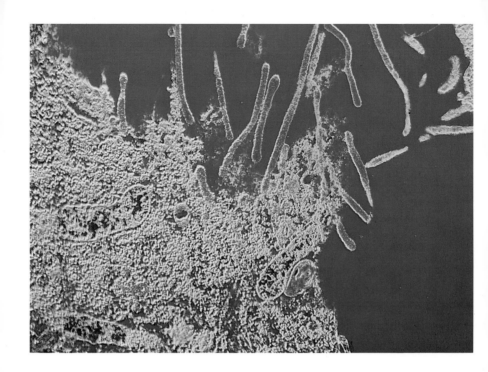

What makes me sick?

The smallest living things are a kind of "germ" that can make you sick. They are the red things attacking one of your cells in the picture. The germ feeds off the cell by breaking it up. When it does this you start feeling sick.

Germs
A germ can be a virus or a bacterium.
A **bacterium** is a "visitor" cell that can live alongside the cells that make up your body.
A **virus** cannot live by itself. To survive, it has to force its way inside the cells that make up your body.

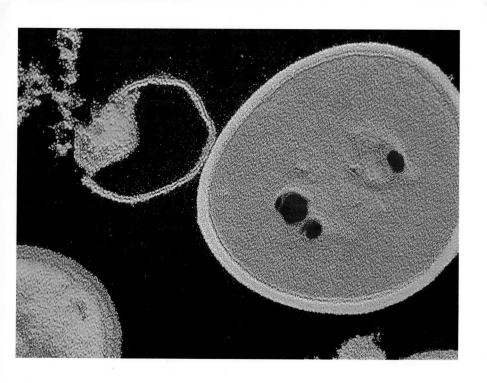

How do I get well?

The bacteria in this picture can also make you sick. Sometimes you need to take antibiotic tablets which break open the outside wall of a bacterium. Once the contents of the cell escape the bacterium dies, and you start feeling well again.

Breeding bacteria
A bacterium can divide itself into two separate bacteria once every twenty minutes. This means that one bacterium is capable of producing 16 million copies of itself in a day.

Inside a cell

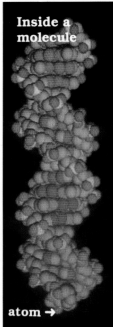

Inside a molecule

atom →

What am I made of?

Your body is made of cells.

Your cells are made of molecules.

Your molecules are made of atoms.

Your atoms are made of a nucleus and some electrons.

The nucleus is made of protons and neutrons.

And your protons and neutrons are made of quarks …